MW00882283

This Journal Belongs To:

____

____

Journals to write in
Positive Party Publishing
SUGAR LAND, TEXAS

[illegible]

[illegible]

[illegible]

[illegible]

Made in the USA
Columbia, SC
04 March 2021

33861551R00068